MY JOURNEY TO FINANCIAL FREEDOM

MY JOURNEY TO FINANCIAL FREEDOM

A memoir of identity, healing, and wealth building

Jacqueline Jarl, Ed.D.

This book is a work of nonfiction. While every effort has been made to ensure that accuracy and timeliness of the information presented, neither the publisher nor the author assumes any responsibility for errors, omissions, or outcomes resulting from the use of this material. This publication is intended for informational purposes only and does not constitute legal, financial, medical, or other professional advice. Readers should consult qualified professionals before making decisions based on the content.

COPYRIGHT @ 2026 JJ's Coaching Services

All Rights Reserved. This book may not be reproduced in whole or in part, stored in a retrieval system, or transmitted in any form or by any means electronic, mechanical, photocopying, recording, or otherwise without prior written permission from the publisher except in the case of brief quotations used in critical articles or reviews.

First Paperback Printing February 2026
Published by JJ's Coaching Services
Sanger, TX, USA

ISBN: 979-8-9947030-0-7

Table of Contents

Introduction i

Chapter 1: From Army to Corporate America: My First Financial Wake-Up Call 1

Chapter 2: Finding My Tribe: The Turning Point 13

Chapter 3: Initiate Journey to Financial Freedom: From Surviving to Strategizing 21

Chapter 4: Mistakes and Setbacks: The Power of Course-Correction 33

Chapter 5: Trauma Healing: The Work Beneath the Work 41

Chapter 6: The Pivot: Untethering from Corporate America 59

Chapter 7: The End Game: Financial Freedom 71

Epilogue 79

Acknowledgements 85

About the Author 87

Introduction

If you had asked me fifteen years ago where I'd be today, I would have given you a well-rehearsed answer. One where I successfully climbed the corporate ladder, purchased my own home, and maybe even had a seven-figure net worth.

But what I wouldn't have told you, because I didn't know it yet, is that none of those things truly defined freedom. Not the title. Not the paycheck. Not even the million-dollar net worth. How do I know now? Because I got all those things during my journey to financial freedom, and none of it actually mattered.

I also wouldn't have told you that in the midst of outward success, I was struggling internally trying to heal from trauma, navigate life after the military, make sense of corporate America, and figure out how to build a financially sound future free from salary dependency. I wouldn't have talked about those things because in my lived experience, vulnerability was not welcome. It was interpreted as weakness. Feelings are not facts. If you felt bad, were sick, or needed a break, you were told, "Life is tough," to be a good soldier and to "suck it up and drive on."

Over the last ten years, I have learned many lessons on my journey to financial freedom, and that is why this book exists. I want people to know that you don't need to invent something to be a millionaire. You don't need to be a social media influencer with hundreds of thousands of followers and paid sponsorships. You

Introduction

don't need to be famous. All you need are intention and discipline, and you too can reach financial freedom. If I, Jacqueline Jarl (JJ), a first-generation immigrant with limited technology skills and no social media presence, can achieve financial freedom in my thirties, you can too.

This book is not a "how to get rich quick" guide, and it does not cover every tip and trick to building wealth. It's not a rags-to-riches story meant to glamorize grind culture. *My Journey to Financial Freedom* is a truth-telling. It's my personal journey to financial freedom through identity struggles, trauma healing, finding the right tribe, and learning about financial literacy and the rules of our financial system here in the United States of America. This book is a blueprint for breaking cycles, reclaiming your power, and living your ideal life, one intentional financial decision at a time.

So, who is this book written for?

It's for military service members who will be transitioning out of the military.

It's for veterans trying to adjust to civilian life and navigate a world that suddenly feels both free and foreign, while trying to heal from military trauma.

It's for the people who are staring at their bank accounts wondering why their six-figure salary still feels like a paycheck-to-paycheck hustle.

It's for those successful, high-achieving professionals who do not feel fulfilled and are not loving life.

It's for people who want to break free from salary dependency and live life on their own terms.

And on a more personal note, it's for the unhealed version of me from 2013.

If I could write myself a note and send it back in time, here's what it would say:

- Healing is just as much a part of wealth-building as cash flow management. If you don't have your health, you don't have anything.
- Finding financial freedom is a process of unlearning and relearning.
- Purpose and peace aren't found in promotions, pay raises, or other people's approval; they're found in living a life that honors your values.

My Journey to Financial Freedom is part memoir, part guide, and part mirror. It started as homework from therapy. The assignment was to journal significant events that shaped me as a human being. You'll read about my goals, my struggles, my breakthroughs, my detours, my mistakes, my wins, and my life lessons. And through it all, I hope you'll find pieces of your own story and maybe even answers to questions you haven't known how to ask.

You deserve a life free from financial stress.
You deserve to own your time, your energy, and your future.
You deserve to thrive, not just survive

Chapter 1
From Army to Corporate America: My First Financial Wake-Up Call

"Before anything else, preparation is the key to success." – Alexander Graham Bell

Transitioning out of the military wasn't something I had fully prepared for—mentally, emotionally, or financially. I didn't leave with a dream job lined up or a six-month emergency fund. Instead, I was medically discharged, had physical and mental health issues, and was uncertain of what the civilian world held for me.

I served as a Military Intelligence Officer in the Army. That title might sound impressive, but unfortunately, it has no directly translatable roles in the civilian world. Translating my military experience often led to people looking at me like I had horns coming out of my head. Many people told me to go work at a three-letter agency or a government contractor, given I still had an active TS/SCI clearance. But at that time, I was so burned out in the Army I did not want to go back to working for the government. I didn't know what I wanted, but I knew a government job was not the answer. And let me tell you, that uncertainty hit fast and hard.

Chapter 1: From Army to Corporate America

After my discharge in December 2013, I found myself broke, with no job prospects. One day I was a captain in the Army and the next I was nobody with no income. I bounced between friends and family for a place to live for a total of seven months, collecting unemployment and a minimal amount of VA disability. Those months were humbling and scary. I had never been in a situation where I was strapped for cash, not because I was rich but because I had been in the military for my entire adult life. I didn't even know where else I could work. I barely had a presentable resume, zero interview practice, and no clue where to even look for corporate jobs.

But JJ, didn't you attend the Army's Transition Assistance Program (TAP)?

Yes, I did. And I didn't learn anything about corporate America. The quality of the transition curriculum was terrible (more a "check the box" for the Army than information that would actually help people get hired) and mostly geared toward junior enlisted and government jobs. There was zero exposure to civilian jobs or how to write a civilian resume. I later found out this was intentional. When I ran the military recruiting department for my civilian corporation, I tried to become a part of the TAP curriculum. Not to advertise my company but to teach transitioning service members about resumes, interviews, salary negotiations, etc. I was told that the government cannot appear to favor any organization, so it cannot have civilian corporations as a part of the TAP curriculum.

Alright, back to my transition. My initial ideal job was to teach English in Taiwan. That was the ultimate plan I set in motion in 2011, when I started my master's degree in teaching, with a focus on Teaching English to Speakers of Other Languages (TESOL). Why Taiwan? Because I lived there for ten years, and that's where my parents immigrated from. In fact, they were living in Taiwan when I separated from the Army. Without a permanent place to live (one of my mom's friends had taken me in for a couple weeks), I figured the best thing to do was to buy a one-way ticket to Taiwan. It was better to move back in with my parents than to continue inconveniencing my mom's friend and her family. I remember thinking I would be a hot commodity (West Point graduate, native English speaker, master's degree in TESOL) for one of the English academies there; somebody will for sure hire me. Also, the only healthcare I had after separation from the Army was at the Veterans Affairs. After visiting twice, I knew I needed better care. Taiwan's healthcare was more advanced, did not require insurance, and was much cheaper than the United States.

After I arrived in Taiwan on a 90-day visa-exempt entry, I realized how naïve I was. I had acted out of desperation and on assumptions. If I didn't know how to get a job in a country where I was authorized to work, why did I think I would have an easier time

Chapter 1: From Army to Corporate America

finding a job in a country where I was *not* authorized to work? But I wasn't going to give up so easily. I started physical therapy to alleviate the physical pain I was experiencing. At the same time, I visited English academies and tutoring companies in person to give them my resume. That's when I found out that recruiting for those types of companies is always done abroad, because they are looking for native English speakers. There is no local recruiting presence. This was clearly described on their websites, which I would have known if I had just done some research before flying across the Pacific Ocean.

Given that news, I shifted my focus to finding work as a private English tutor. Again, with my credentials, I assumed I could make good money tutoring kids from wealthy families. However, most of those families already had tutors who were experienced teachers at the local American or international schools. No parent would fire their tenured, trusted educators for a young and inexperienced ex-soldier. After six months of making no headway (yes, I did have to leave the country and re-enter so I wouldn't overstay the 90-day exempt visa), I decided it was time to return to the United States and try to find employment.

I arrived back in California in May 2014, and it felt like I had stepped into a paused movie. Nothing had changed. I was still unemployed, still without job prospects, and still clueless about how to even begin applying for corporate jobs. I was back living with my mom's friend, who had taken me in when I first separated from the military. It was like déjà vu. My confidence had evaporated. In a moment of desperation, I pulled out the *newspaper*. Yes, the actual, crinkly, ink-smudged paper, because it was the only place I knew for sure that listed job openings. I came across an ad for a teaching position at a local daycare and decided to apply. When I arrived for the interview, they explained the role: a $40,000 salary, some teaching, but mostly babysitting, changing diapers, and cleaning up after the kids. It was clear this wasn't my area of expertise and definitely not what I had in mind for my career. I then applied for the English teaching opportunities I'd once considered in Taiwan. When the offers came back at $25,000 a year (full-time roles in Taiwan), I knew that I would need to live with my parents or a relative if I accepted those offers, and I was not interested in doing that.

So I put on a fake smile for my mom's friend, laughed at dinner, and acted like I had things under control. But at night, lying awake, my mind spun. *What if I never find a job that pays enough? What if I'm still living with my parents in my thirties? What if this is all there is for me now?* The questions felt heavier than the silence in my room. I started to wonder if I should have pushed through my injuries, burnout, and mental health issues to stay in the military. At least I would still have an income.

Chapter 1: From Army to Corporate America

It was at this time that I decided to change career tracks. While I loved to teach, I prioritized survival over passion. I opened Google search and typed "jobs for former Military Intelligence Officers" into the search bar, clinging to the hope that some perfect position was out there waiting for me. But I didn't even know what I was looking for—what I could do in the civilian world. Out of desperation, I signed up with a recruiting agency. It was at no charge, so I figured it couldn't hurt. They fixed my resume and gave me some interview tips over the phone. Then they asked, "What type of company do you want to work for?" There was a long, awkward silence, and then I responded with, "What do you mean? I can choose?"

In the military, jobs are assigned. You're told where to go, what to do, what to wear, and for how long. They would occasionally ask for your preferences, but the needs of the Army always trumped your preferences. Having a say in my career, choosing a path instead of being directed down one, was a brand-new concept.

After some thought, I told them that I wanted to work for a company that made products that were *needed* by society instead of merely *wanted* by society. The example I gave them of a product that was wanted and not needed was the smartphone. I did not own a smartphone until I was already a lieutenant in the Army, so I know you can live without one. I specifically called out the smartphone because I am fluent in Mandarin and I did not want the agency to hit the easy button and send me to tech companies in Silicon Valley that ran their supply chains out of Asia. Another criterion was that I wanted the company to contribute to the greater good by giving back to society. The agent who was working with me immediately said, "Oh, you need to go med device." Having never heard of that industry before, I said, "Sure, what are my next steps?"

Within two weeks, I received my first corporate job offer. I grabbed it like a lifeline…because it was. The agency representative called me to let me know I would be getting an offer and that what the recruiter wants to hear is, "Yes, I accept." Like a good soldier, I did as I was told. After all, they've gotten me this far, and the offer was twice what I was getting when I tried on my own. No research, no questions, no counteroffers or negotiations. Compensation was not negotiable in the military, so it didn't even cross my mind that I could ask for more. Seriously, I didn't even get a sign-on bonus. I was just grateful someone was willing to take a chance on me and give me a job. That lack of confidence and information caused me to be underemployed and underpaid—terms I didn't even know existed at that time.

After I started in corporate America, I thought I was finally making it. I was earning a steady paycheck, had my own healthcare plan, and had moved into my own apartment. I had everything I needed, or so I thought. This must be what people mean when they

Chapter 1: From Army to Corporate America

say, "living the dream." At least that's what I told myself I was doing.

It didn't take long for the cracks to show. The dream quickly vanished after two colleagues were laid off due to restructuring. The organization decided that instead of the mechanical engineering roles it currently had, it needed two electrical engineering roles. This shook me to my core. In the military, your paycheck was guaranteed as long as you didn't break the law. There was structure. There was predictability. There was honor in service. Nobody lost their paychecks. If the organization no longer needed you in your position, you simply got reassigned to a different role or a different unit, but your paycheck was not at risk. This was not true in corporate America due to at-will employment. The organization can terminate your employment at any time, for no reason. It felt like I was a number on a spreadsheet. And for the first time, I realized that a "steady" paycheck wasn't the security blanket I thought it was. The very thing that had made me feel "safe" was actually quite fragile. That illusion of stability shattered the moment I saw how quickly things could change, and it brought back all the emotions of "captain one day, nobody the next." I knew that to prevent myself from being broke again and to have true control of my life, I could not depend on a corporate salary or income that's controlled by people who only care about the bottom line. This was the first spark that lit the fire on my journey to financial freedom.

Transitioning from military to corporate was one of the toughest times of my life—physically, mentally, and emotionally. But it laid the foundation for everything I've learned about financial freedom. It taught me that freedom doesn't start with a paycheck—it starts with knowledge, preparation, and belief in your worth. It begins when you stop waiting to be chosen and start choosing yourself. I didn't have all the answers back then, but I had the will to learn. And from that will came growth, confidence, and eventually, a vision for a thriving life enabled by financial freedom.

Lessons from my journey to financial freedom:

Figure out what *you* want. The civilian world is wide open, and you're in charge now. The world is your oyster, and the sky is the limit. You get to pick the company, the location, and the job. That freedom is powerful, but you have to decide *how* you want to live your life before you start chasing opportunities. Otherwise, you'll end up living someone else's dream instead of your own. Get clear on your priorities, your non-negotiables, and your vision. Then, protect that vision fiercely. Don't let other people's opinions or expectations pull you off course.

Start early. If you're transitioning out of the military or even just thinking about it, start preparing long before your separation date. Don't wait until the last few weeks to scramble. Begin networking at least twelve months out. Six months before separation, start

Chapter 1: From Army to Corporate America

practicing interviews so you can show up to interviews confidently three months out, with the goal of having an offer in hand before your final day in uniform. Remember, you can always negotiate a later start date, but you can't negotiate if you don't have an offer. Tap into every free resource available to transitioning service members. They exist for a reason. Use them to your advantage.

Find mentors. The fastest way to learn is from those who've already walked the path. Seek out veterans who've successfully transitioned to civilian careers. They can help you avoid costly mistakes and blind spots. LinkedIn is your friend in this situation. Be bold. Reach out to other veterans who work at your target companies/industries and ask for thirty minutes on their calendar. Come ready with questions. In my experience, veterans are almost always willing to help other veterans; it's part of our DNA. But the opportunity only comes if you ask.

Research before you act. Don't assume and don't settle. Research companies, how they hire, pay bands, culture, etc. Make sure the company's values are aligned with your values, culture, and long-term goals. A shiny, new offer with a higher salary will tempt you, but it might pull you away from your purpose and might not be the best long-term fit. Learn the details before you act because acting too fast is going to cost you time, money, and potentially your ideal career.

Negotiate everything. Corporations are running profitable businesses. They will never offer you the highest possible compensation on the first go-around. Every extra dollar they pay you is an extra dollar taken away from their profit line. Professionally, ask for a higher salary, an annual bonus, a sign-on bonus, vacation days, **everything!** You never know what corporations are willing to give if you don't ask.

A corporate salary does not provide financial stability. Contrary to popular belief, a corporate paycheck is not stability, regardless of how "steady" it might seem. It gives the illusion of stability, but it's fragile. At-will employment means you can be laid off at any time, with little notice. True financial stability comes when your income doesn't depend on someone else's decision to employ you. Learn financial literacy and create multiple streams of income. Always pay yourself and your future self first. Your corporate job can be taken away at any moment. Your skills, your network, and your ability to create income are your real safety net.

Chapter 2
Finding My Tribe: The Turning Point

"You are the average of the five people you spend the most time with." – Jim Rohn

After landing my first corporate job and moving into my own apartment, you'd think I was finally on the right track: a great job with a Fortune 500 company, independent living, a steady paycheck. From the outside, it looked like I was winning. But the truth? I was unraveling. Slowly. Quietly. And dangerously.

At work, I wore the mask well. Polished. Professional. High performing. I checked every corporate box and put on such a good show that nobody suspected anything was wrong. I knew how to play the role. Years in the Army had taught me how to push down pain, compartmentalize emotions, and keep moving for the mission. I had mastered survival mode.

But after 5:00 p.m., when the badge came off and the front door closed behind me, I fell apart. I wasn't thriving. I wasn't even living. I was barely functioning.

How bad was it? I was twenty-eight years old and still eating pizza rolls and ramen for dinner. Every night. Not because I loved

Chatper 2: Finding My Tribe

them, but because I didn't have the energy or the mental capacity to care for myself properly. All my effort went into holding it together at work. When I got home, there was nothing left. No mental bandwidth. No emotional reserve. Just exhaustion and emptiness.

And the weekends? They were worse. They revolved around partying. Endless bar tabs, brunches, and bottomless mimosas. It wasn't about the fun. It was about chasing community and connection, trying to fill that dark void inside me. From the outside, it looked like I was social, popular, even thriving. But the truth was sobering: most of those so-called "friends" only hung around because I bought them shots or never let them walk into a bar alone. They weren't there for me. They were there for what I could provide for them.

I remember when I hung out with them, I would often become the subject of their entertainment. They would often bring up the fact that I did not know much about the civilian world. And every time a new topic came up, and I didn't know it, they would laugh and say something to the effect of: "You don't know about that? Have you been living in a cave? You're like a newborn baby."

And when I stopped providing, when I stopped picking up the tab and stopped always saying yes, the calls and texts stopped too. The silence was deafening. And the void inside me only grew darker.

I was in a dark place. One of the darkest, if I'm completely honest. I refused to acknowledge my unresolved mental health issues from the Army. (I wouldn't get help until 2020, seven long years later. More on that later.) And because I ignored it, my pain found other ways to manifest itself. I stopped enjoying life. In fact, I started actively testing limits. Doing reckless things that could've easily ended my life or landed me in serious trouble with the law. Looking back, I realize it was a loud, desperate cry for help. A twisted way of saying: somebody please see me. Please notice I'm not okay.

And then there were the moments no one knew about—the moments that haunt me even now. Quiet, drunken moments when I'd get behind the wheel, bitter, and thinking to myself, maybe today is the day. Maybe today I finally crash and the suffering ends. Not because I actually wanted to die, but because I couldn't see the point of living the way I was living. Death had to be better. At least I wouldn't be here to deal with the aftermath.

I didn't have goals. I didn't have dreams. I was just…existing. Floating. Every month I overspent ($80,000 in San Jose, CA doesn't stretch far when you're living recklessly) and had to pull money from what little savings I had from unemployment checks. Every month when I had to dig into my savings, I told myself, "I'll worry about it next month…if I'm still here." The little bit of savings I had from those seven months of unemployment was gone within the first few months of starting a full-time job. Not on anything meaningful. Not on investments. Not even on memories that mattered. It

Chatper 2: Finding My Tribe

vanished into bottles, nights out, and mindless spending, all in an attempt to earn approval from people who didn't care about me.

But the money wasn't the real issue. It was a symptom of something much deeper.

That's the part that's hardest to admit. It wasn't just about being broke. It wasn't just about being lost. It was about being completely out of alignment. I wasn't living my values. I wasn't honoring my purpose. And that disconnect ate away at me, piece by piece, day after day. I was showing up to a life I didn't even recognize, much less like. And when you live a lie that big, when you betray yourself that deeply, it chips away at your worth. It steals your hope. It robs you of your sense of meaning.

Then, in March 2015, everything shifted.

My manager invited me to her bachelorette party in Las Vegas and wedding in Jamaica. At the time, it felt like just another social obligation. I mean, who says "no" to their boss's invites? And I hadn't been to Jamaica before, so I figured it could serve as a vacation as well. But these two trips turned out to be turning points and changed my life forever.

Including my manager, I met three women at these two events who would become my tribe (although I already knew my manager, I did not know her outside of work. The bachelorette and wedding were where I met her as a person, not as a manager). Three strong, confident, grounded women who saw me. Not the polished mask I wore at work, not the girl buying shots at the bar. Me. The real me. And the most shocking part? They accepted me as I was. They were the first people who made me feel included—like I belonged.

For the bachelorette party, I had purchased a pair of four-inch peep-toe heels to go with my outfit. However, I really did not have experience wearing heels and did not know how to walk properly in them. To illustrate, years later, when this event came back up, the ladies described it as "a baby giraffe learning how to walk for the first time." Once they saw how I was moving in these heels, without judgment or laughter, they gave me a lesson right there in the hotel room. They were encouraging, and when I finally got it right, they cheered so loudly you would have thought they had won the jackpot in the casino downstairs.

With them, I didn't have to pretend I had it all together. I didn't have to buy their approval. I didn't even have to spend every waking moment with them as we all live in different parts of the country and would meet up once or twice a year. But the trips were meaningful, inspiring, and healing. We talked about what was going well, what was not going well, and what we needed to do to live our ideal lives. Having this group of ladies enabled me in my healing process. This was the first time in my life that I felt okay not to be perfect. That it was normal not to be like other people. They gave me the freedom to exist and heal, on my own terms, broken pieces and all.

Chatper 2: Finding My Tribe

The best part was they didn't try to fix me. They didn't judge me. They didn't demand more than I could give. Instead, they simply stood beside me quietly, patiently, and with unconditional love. They showed me what real friendship looks like: it doesn't require money, or partying, or always being their plus-one. They showed me what it means to be supported without strings attached.

What struck me most about them was how they lived with intention. They talked about their goals, their dreams, their futures. Not as if it were some far-off fantasy, but as if it were already in motion. And the thing is, they backed it up. They didn't just talk about it. They lived it. They breathed it. And they made those dreams come true.

Being around them sparked something inside me. Something I hadn't felt in years: hope, possibility, and a light at the end of a tunnel for the darkness I was experiencing. For the first time in a long time, I started to see my worth again. I started to believe that maybe I was more than my productivity at work. Maybe I was more than my paycheck and title. Maybe I was worthy simply because I existed.

That shift changed everything. Instead of "To live is to suffer," it's now "Life is a gift." I stopped surviving and started thinking about what it might mean to thrive. And the first step in that journey was accountability and ownership. Starting with the thing that was bleeding into every area of my life: my finances.

That's when my real journey to financial freedom began. Not just in dollars, but in mindset, in alignment, and in purpose.

Because here's the truth: Financial freedom isn't about money. It's about being free from the lies you tell yourself and the lies that society tells us. It's about being free from the people who drain you and developing the ability to say no. It's about being free from the patterns that keep you stuck. And it's about being free from the trauma you've dealt with for so long that it's become the norm.

My tribe reminded me of who I am. They led me back to my confidence, my self-worth, and my value. Through how they lived, they inspired me to fight for my purpose and to become who I'm meant to be.

Lessons from my journey to financial freedom:

Find your tribe: You will become a reflection of the people you spend the most time with, whether you realize it or not. If your circle is negative, stagnant, or careless with money, those traits will seep into your life. But when you surround yourself with people who are living intentionally, people who are chasing growth, holding themselves accountable, and encouraging you to do the same, you'll start to rise with them. The right tribe will challenge you when you're slacking, celebrate you when you win, and pick you back up when life knocks you down. The wrong tribe will keep you small

Chatper 2: Finding My Tribe

and broke. The right tribe will change your life. Choose carefully. Your future depends on it.

You are worthy: Your worth is not tied to your job title, your salary, or what anyone else thinks of you. It doesn't depend on the approval of a boss, a partner, or society. It's not up for negotiation. Your worth comes from who you are, your character, your values, and your resilience. When you truly believe that you are enough, you stop settling for less. You stop accepting crumbs when you deserve the whole loaf. You stop hiding parts of yourself so you can fit in. You stop spending money just so you can be "seen". And when you stand in that truth, you become unstoppable, not because life gets easier, but because you finally understand you were worthy all along.

Find your purpose: Your past is not a prison sentence; it's a classroom. It may shape you, but it does not define you. Every single day is a fresh opportunity to decide where your life goes next. Maybe you've been drifting. Maybe you've been following a path someone else chose for you. That doesn't mean you have to stay on that path. It's never too late to pivot, to choose differently, to start living intentionally and with purpose. The moment you start aligning your actions with what truly matters to you, that's when life starts to feel like it's yours again.

Chapter 3
Initiate Journey to Financial Freedom: From Surviving to Strategizing

"A big part of financial freedom is having your heart and mind free from worry about the what-ifs of life." – Suze Orman

My first year in corporate America taught me one of the most important lessons of my life: just because you are earning doesn't mean you are progressing. I thought having a steady paycheck was the finish line. That I'd made it. But in reality, I was just staying afloat. Bills, rent, and social "obligations" drained my account as fast as that paycheck hit. I wasn't building wealth; I was just surviving.

That's when it hit me: The status quo wasn't going to work for me. Without new mindsets and habits, I would always be stuck in the poverty cycle, living paycheck to paycheck. I needed a new path, one that actually led somewhere.

Chapter 3: Initiate Journey to Financial Freedom

One of the first things that I did after meeting my tribe was define what mattered to me—my **values**. Before I could build wealth, I had to understand *why* I wanted it. What was driving me? For me, it came down to three core values:

1. Integrity: I wanted to win, but I wanted to win the right way. No shortcuts. No schemes. No dependence on luck. Just honest, intentional work.
2. Service: I've always been wired to help others—my best days in the military weren't when I was rated as the top officer in my peer group or when I got an award. It was when I was able to help a soldier with their housing situation or when I mentored another officer. I feel most fulfilled when I'm helping others live their best lives.
3. Freedom: I wanted to have full control of my life. My military career showed me what it's like not to have a say in your job and where you work. You get the orders, and you follow those orders. In the corporate world, if a company decides you are no longer needed as an employee, you could be out on the street. I wanted to be free to make life decisions that were best for me, not best for my wallet.

With my values clear, I could finally see the *why* behind the *what*. There was now a road map to where I wanted to go. And that meant it was time to set **goals**.

Setting goals is easy, and we do it all the time. But more often than not, those goals never see the light of day (think New Year's resolutions). Setting *meaningful* goals—the kind that pull you out of bed on hard days and push you through seasons of sacrifice—is where the rubber meets the road. I had to get brutally honest with myself and ask: *What do I want my life to look like?* Not what I thought I should want. Not what others expected of me. But what *I* truly desired. After some soul-searching, I came up with three goals:

1. **Buy a home before age thirty.** I craved stability. This is partly because of my experience of having to live with friends and relatives after leaving the Army and also because I was tired of the uncertainty that came with renting and having to move every year because my rent was increasing by the legal maximum (10% annually in California). Each move was stressful and costly. I wanted to change things without asking permission and create a space that was mine. A home, to me, symbolized security, stability, progress, and freedom from the whims of a landlord.

2. **Achieve financial freedom before age forty.** I didn't want to spend the best years of my life stuck in a job I didn't love, counting down the days to the weekend or dreading Mondays. I wanted choices. I wanted to go on vacation without asking for permission. I wanted the freedom to walk away from any job, company, or environment (personal or

professional) that didn't serve me and align with my values. I didn't want to be chained to a paycheck. Financial independence, to me, was essential so I could reclaim full ownership of my time and live my ideal life.

3. **Travel to one new country or three new states annually.** I wanted to learn about other cultures and expand my perspective beyond the bubble I had grown up in. The military sent me to Arizona, Korea, Georgia (the state), Jordan, and Kuwait, and I loved immersing myself in those new cultures. Those experiences opened my eyes and sparked a deeper curiosity about the world. Experiencing new places, people, and ways of life was an investment in myself, not just for the memories, but for personal growth. Every trip was a reminder that the world has so much to offer, and that there were countless ways to live, work, and find meaning.

Setting these goals gave me direction, clarity, and purpose. They helped me filter my decisions through a long-term lens. Every "yes" or "no" started to align with the bigger picture. I call this my North Star. Having a North Star allowed me to say "yes" only to the things that were going to help me reach my goals. It kept me from getting distracted by "shiny objects" along the way. And trust me, there will always be *a lot* of "shiny objects" along the journey. But if you stay disciplined and say "no" to everything that isn't aligned with your North Star, your ideal life will start to fall into place.

Now that I had my North Star, I knew dreaming wasn't enough. I needed a **plan** that was grounded in reality and aligned with the life I envisioned. The three goals I set were bold, life-changing goals. And that meant I had to treat them seriously. I began breaking each goal down into smaller, achievable steps with six-month milestones. I researched financial literacy, tracked my spending, increased my corporate income, decreased taxes, and stayed focused even when the progress felt slow. I celebrated small wins along the way because they were evidence that I was getting closer.

For my first goal of buying a house before thirty, I started house hunting in California, thinking I'd plant roots in my home state. But the deeper I got into the numbers, the more the truth became impossible to ignore: Buying a home there would leave me house-poor. Sure, I could technically afford a mortgage with the VA loan at 0% down and no private mortgage interest, but it would stretch me so thin that I'd be sacrificing my second and third goals just to keep a roof over my head. I wouldn't be able to live life the way I wanted, which included travel. Heck, I probably wouldn't even be able to afford furniture for that house. That's not freedom; that's a trap.

So I pulled out my spreadsheets, did the math, and had a hard but honest conversation with myself: *If I stay in California, I won't hit*

Chapter 3: Initiate Journey to Financial Freedom

my goals. Not in the timeframe I've set. Probably not ever. That realization hurt. But it also gave me clarity on next steps. After a lot of reflection, I made a life-altering decision: I needed to leave California.

This move wasn't just about escaping high housing prices but more about positioning myself strategically for the life I wanted to build. I was looking for a state that offered strong veteran benefits, no state income tax, and an overall environment that would support my journey to financial freedom while still allowing me to live fully while on the journey. After reviewing my company's locations, two stood out: Texas and Florida.

Per company policy, I first shared my intentions with my manager, then I started combing through the internal job board. That's when I spotted an opening in our Dallas, Texas office on one of our sister teams. The role was the same title and grade as my current position, and I already had a relationship with the hiring manager. The process took about a month, including a trip to the Texas office for in-person interviews. On December 23, 2015, I received the offer. I remember I had just landed in Taiwan to visit my parents for the holidays and noticed a voicemail from the hiring manager to give her a call back (she called me while I was in flight). That holiday season was extra special because I knew, with the acceptance of the Texas position, that my dream life was starting to take shape. Less than two months later, in February 2016, I packed up my life and headed to Texas, ready to step into the next chapter of both my career and my journey to financial freedom.

This one decision drastically changed my financial outlook. For the first time ever, I could actually see myself reaching my North Star and living my ideal life. Here are some examples of immediate financial gains I experienced after moving to Texas:

- Increase in net income due to no state income tax—my salary and bonus stayed the same which meant savings of approximately $400 per month. $400 per month invested at a 6% rate of return (S&P 500 returned on average 10% over the last 10 years) over 30 years is $390,000.
- Decrease in cost of living—using gas as an example: It was $30 cheaper per fill-up, and I filled up twice a month, so that was a savings of $720 per year. Applying the same logic for groceries, utilities, dining out, etc., I was netting thousands of dollars a year.
- No bar tabs—I didn't know anyone in Texas which saved me ~$200/month that I used to spend on alcohol and eating out.

But additional cash doesn't mean anything if you don't put it to work. And I did not have the proper financial education to build wealth. Literally, in my twenty-eight years of life, nobody had ever talked to me about money management and how to grow my money. The advice was always: you need a Certified Financial Planner. I

Chapter 3: Initiate Journey to Financial Freedom

refused to believe that I needed to depend on someone else to grow my money. So I started deep diving into financial literacy using free resources on the internet. And here's what came out of the self-education that enabled me to start working toward goals #2 and #3:

- Established positive monthly cash flow: I started to track every dollar in and every dollar out on a free Excel template. No more guessing. No more hoping I don't overspend. I did have a budget initially, but I learned that budgets don't work for me. Because the more I restricted myself the more I wanted to spend (I guess it's my rebellious side). This is when I learned cash flow management. I didn't put restrictions on how much I could spend on each category of spending (shopping, dining, etc.). Instead, I managed my overall cash flow. And I adjusted my spending to match my values and goals—instead of spending money on frivolous things, I spent money on things that would value add to my life and make me happy, like travel.
- Paid myself first: I started to move money directly from my paycheck into savings and investments. Since that money never hit my checking account, I couldn't spend it. Now that I was tracking my expenses, I knew exactly how much my nondiscretionary spending (mortgage, bills, groceries) was per month. What's left over is what I can use for discretionary spending. And I can spend it on anything I wanted, guilt free. When I got raises and promotions, I

avoided lifestyle creep and increased the amount that went into savings and investments.

- Built an emergency fund: Before investing, before big purchases, I made sure I had a safety net equal to six months of living expenses. To be transparent, this took some time to build since I was a single-income household and didn't really have any savings. But once I got there, it gave me peace of mind, flexibility, and the opportunity to take calculated risks and grow my portfolio even more.

- Maxed out retirement accounts: I took full advantage of my 401(k) with employer match, Roth IRA, and HSA. I didn't just throw money into investment accounts; I spent time learning about the market, its history, mutual funds, and ETFs, and created a simple low-cost portfolio that would get me to my North Star over time.

- Learned about other ways to build wealth: Real estate, side hustles, reward credit cards, passive income—I learned it all. Not everything was a good fit for what I was trying to build and some things were just too complicated and beyond my knowledge. But I figured the more I learned, the more I would be in control of what should or should not be a part of my portfolio. Learning never stops as there are always new opportunities and ways to build wealth.

This part of the journey wasn't about being perfect. I doubted myself daily and had imposter syndrome (who am I to think I can build wealth on my own?). But I always went back to my North Star and stayed focused on the goals. Winning was measured by progress, not perfection. As long as my net worth was growing month after month, even if it was only by $1, I considered it a win.

Somewhere along the way, I noticed a shift: I wasn't just surviving anymore. I was thriving. Instead of flying economy on international flights, I could afford the lay-flat business class seats. I didn't worry about running out of money or being laid off because I had a surplus every month and a fully funded emergency fund. My decisions were no longer driven by the number in my bank accounts. If I didn't go to a social event, it was because I didn't want to, not because I couldn't afford to. Every year, my discretionary income and net worth increased. I was getting a taste of my ideal life and what it felt like to have complete ownership of that life.

Lessons from my journey to financial freedom:

Where you grew up might not be the best place for you to build your life. As humans, we're naturally drawn to what feels familiar and comfortable, but comfort doesn't always equal progress. The city, town, or neighborhood your parents chose may have been the right place for them, but that doesn't mean it's the right place for you to reach your full potential or achieve your goals. Sometimes, building the life you truly want requires stepping away from the familiar and planting yourself in an environment that aligns with your vision.

Look for a company that includes equity in your offer letter or a bomb 401(k) match plan. When it comes to your career, be intentional about more than just salary. Look for companies that include equity in their offers and/or provide a strong 401(k) match. I realize not all employers do this, so believe in your value and aim to find one that does. Stocks and retirement contributions are powerful wealth-building tools, especially when it's other people's money that ends up in your accounts. When your employer is giving you stocks—either through restricted stock units, options, or 401(k) matching—it's wealth that you don't have to work extra hours for and don't have to buy with your own money. Over time, these benefits will be life changing.

Your emergency fund comes before investments. I know it's tempting to jump straight into building wealth with stocks, real estate, crypto, you name it. But here's the truth: Without an emergency fund, your financials will topple easily. Life will happen. The car will break down, the water heater will quit, and unexpected medical issues will come out of nowhere. And when it does, if you don't have that emergency fund as a safety net, you'll end up going into debt, most likely using credit cards and paying 20-30% interest. Other options include pulling from your retirement accounts prematurely, potentially losing out on decades of compound interest, not to mention the mandatory government fees for early withdrawals. Your emergency fund is what keeps you from sliding backward the moment life throws a curveball. And trust me, life will always throw curveballs. Emergency funds are not exciting or sexy, but they're the structural support that allow every other part of your wealth-building plan to stand strong. Investments build wealth, your emergency fund protects it.

Financial literacy is key! Above all, remember this: Financial literacy is the foundation of wealth. Money is only a tool. It's never only about the money itself; it's about knowing what to do with it, how to make it work for you, and how to use it to create freedom. When you understand how to manage your finances, you gain control over your life. And that control frees you from financial stress and living on anyone else's terms.

Chapter 4
Mistakes and Setbacks: The Power of Course-Correction

"Do the one thing you think you cannot do. Fail at it. Try again. Do better the second time. The only people who never tumble are those who never mount the high wire. This is your moment. Own it." – Oprah Winfrey

One of the biggest myths I believed early on was that financial freedom was a straight, predictable path. Save a little, invest a little, and one day you wake up rich and peaceful. Spoiler alert: It doesn't work that way. Progress, *real* progress, requires risk. Not reckless risk, but calculated, uncomfortable, growth-oriented risk.

One of the first things I did after moving to Texas (which was a huge risk in itself, moving to a state that I've never lived in and where I didn't know anyone) was purchase my first primary residence. I had a budget of $350,000…but I didn't stick to it. I ended up purchasing for $358,000. I mean, $8000 over the course of thirty years shouldn't make THAT big of a difference, right?

Chapter 4: Mistakes and Setbacks

WRONG. But the house was perfect (so I thought)—a beautiful new build in a high-end golf course community (which matched where I lived growing up). Great amenities (three pools, two gyms, social events, manicured lawns, etc.) and a zip code I was proud to say out loud. It finally felt like I was where I belonged. But a couple months after close, I was overspending again (at this point, I was making ~$94,000), even with all the savings I had by moving to Texas.

The HOA fees were steep. The school district taxes were high (I don't have kids). And though I loved the home, the expenses didn't love me back. For the first couple months, I made excuses and told myself I'm still in the "moving phase" and continued spending more money. I remember telling myself, "These are onetime expenses, I won't be paying them again." But there were always more onetime expenses that just kept sneaking up on me. After six months, I stopped re-categorizing onetime expenses and the expense tracker showed me what I already knew—I was overstretched.

That meant it was time to make a choice: shrink my lifestyle and cut expenses, or increase my income. If you recall my goals, it was important to me to travel and see the world. But travel was really the only discretionary spending I had (I'm not attracted to material things like jewelry, bags, or shoes). The whole reason I moved to Texas was to prevent me from being house poor. And now here I am, house poor because I didn't stick to my budget and didn't account for all the additional expenses that came with owning a home. I did have the option to not max out my retirement investments, but I was not willing to do that as that would push back my financial freedom date and potentially miss achieving goal #2. It was a great lesson in home ownership and just how expensive it is to own a home.

Being my stubborn self, I refused to give up travel. So I chose to earn more income and picked up a second job as a hostess at a local restaurant. After long days at my corporate job (this is when I was still working in the office five days a week), I'd head straight into the dinner rush and be on my feet for hours greeting guests, managing waitlists, wiping down menus, and rolling silverware. It was humbling. Exhausting. And absolutely necessary to fix a mistake I had made in my financial planning by buying this house.

Working at the restaurant was a blessing in disguise. It stripped away any lingering ego I had about the type of work I was "supposed" to be doing. It taught me that money earned with intention, even when it comes through hard, unglamorous work, is still a step forward. And it reaffirmed a truth I now live by: Short-term discomfort is worth enduring if it protects your long-term vision.

It also opened my eyes in ways I didn't expect. These are what I call life lessons. Prior to this experience, I had only been exposed to corporate salaried or commission-based work. I did not have a full understanding of what it meant to earn variable pay by the hour. To

Chapter 4: Mistakes and Setbacks

clock in and out. To feel every minute of your shift in your body. To hear coworkers talk about not getting enough tips to make rent. It gave me deep respect for the millions of people who do this every day, often with no end in sight. I knew I had an exit strategy, and that this was short term. But for my colleagues at the restaurant, this was their life. What's worse is that they didn't have any resources to help them build a better life. This realization was the initial spark that put me on the path to becoming a financial freedom coach.

About six months later, I got my annual merit increase, and no longer needed the additional income from the restaurant. Once I stabilized my cash flow, it was time to move onto the next step of my financial freedom journey: creating alternate income sources. Having just worked two jobs simultaneously, I knew I did not want to work more. So my target was passive income. I didn't jump in blindly. I took my time, did the research, asked people, and ultimately decided on real estate investing.

Real estate investment was complex. There were so many options—short-term rentals, long-term rentals, flips, REITs, etc. I joined real estate groups on social media, talked with experienced and successful investors, and made a move that felt both bold and responsible: I decided to purchase a single-family residential property outside the largest military base in the contiguous United States in cash and use it as a long-term rental.

Why purchase in cash? Because this type of investment was new to me and I really didn't know what was going to happen. Were there going to be more "onetime expenses" with this property? How long would it take to rent out? Having to pay for another mortgage plus expenses without rental income did not seem like a good idea. Also, if things didn't work out, I wanted to be able to walk away without the added weight of a loan.

Why long-term rentals? Because I wanted to make sure that I would not need to depend on someone else to get a return, such as flips (contractors) and short-term rentals (property management, cleaning crew, etc.). Also, long-term rentals provided more predictability and stability for monthly income.

Why around military installations? Based on my conversations, the vacancy rate appeared to be lower around military installations. I chose this particular military installation for two reasons. 1. It was within driving distance from where I lived. If something were to go wrong, I could easily drive there and take care of issues. 2. The chances of this military installation closing were slim to none so there would always be housing needs with the soldiers getting stationed there. If long-term rentals didn't work out, it would not take long to sell the property.

After the research, at the end of 2018, I liquidated an underperforming investment portfolio that was returning only 4% (S&P 500 returned ~32% between 2013-2018). I got a good deal

Chapter 4: Mistakes and Setbacks

purchasing the primary home of a realtor who was getting married and combining residences with his future wife. This officially marked the beginning of my real estate investment journey.

A year in, the property was performing well. Stable tenant, steady rent, positive cash flow. I started to have a lot of discretionary spending and realized that financial freedom wasn't just a concept anymore, it was coming true right before my eyes.

I doubled down.

I did a cash-out refinance on that first property. With interest rates still low, I was able to pull out equity while keeping the monthly payments low. I used a portion of that cash as a down payment for a second investment property and split the rest between maxing out my Roth IRA and opening a new non-retirement brokerage account (I had extra money that I needed to invest but couldn't put it into retirement because I was already maxed out). While I didn't know it at the time, this brokerage account would later become my long-term care and medical contingency account.

The refinance taught me the power of leverage—using one smart decision to fuel the next. But more than anything, it showed me the importance of stepping outside of your comfort zone to achieve a bigger vision. There is risk in everything unknown, but calculated risks are necessary to advance from the status quo. I now have three rental properties that supplement my monthly income by over

$4,500. If I had let fear of the unknown drive my decisions, I would still have that 4% underperforming portfolio.

Taking risks isn't about being fearless. It's about being brave enough to believe in the research, calculations, and what you're building, even when the path feels uncertain. You don't know what you don't know and sometimes, your calculations are going to falter and that's ok. You can't predict the future. But if you always have a Plan B and know that you might need to pivot, you will be able to figure out what you need to do to correct course and get back on track.

Lessons from my journey to financial freedom:

Don't set goals with arbitrary timelines. I made the mistake of being obsessed with buying a home before I turned thirty. It was partly because of trauma and partly to feed my own ego (look at how successful I am, I can afford my own house!). The milestone became more important than the reasoning behind it. Looking back, the "by when" shouldn't have mattered more than the "why." If I had rented a smaller apartment for those four years instead of stretching myself into homeownership, I would be much wealthier today.

A house costs more than just your mortgage, taxes, and insurance. Your mortgage, taxes, and insurance are just the starting point. Homeownership comes with a steady stream of additional

Chapter 4: Mistakes and Setbacks

expenses such as repairs, maintenance, and decorations that renters rarely have to worry about. Those costs can quietly eat away at your progress and delay your path to financial freedom if you don't account for them in your financial planning.

Growth doesn't happen in comfort, but you have to calculate the risk. There's a fine line between bold and reckless. Don't let fear make your decisions for you. Explore options. Do the research. Ask the hard questions. Run the numbers. Run the numbers again. And again. And *then* make your move. Stretch yourself out of your comfort zone and you will be amazed at the results you can achieve.

Start earlier! I can't say this enough. Compound interest is the most important factor in wealth building. But compound interest doesn't work without *time*. Every year you delay is a year of lost compounding. For example, if you have an investment balance of $100,000 at 30 and never put another dollar into investments, at 6% growth, you will have over $768,000 at 65. But if you waited to invest and have $100,000 invested at 40, you would only have a little over $429,000 at 65. I wish I had learned about real estate investments while I was in the military so I could have started building toward financial freedom at the age of twenty-three instead of twenty-nine. It's never too early to start planning for your financial freedom!

Chapter 5
Trauma Healing: The Work Beneath the Work

"Emotional trauma can have a big impact on our lives, and it's often insidious, showing no overt signs of pathology. Yet, overcoming it might be one of the most powerful things we can do to improve the quality of our lives." – Dr. Peter Attia

Did I forget to mention that I met my partner in September 2018? Oops, haha. Craig and I met at Corporate Challenge, a charity event our company participated in, benefiting the Special Olympics. We were both on the bowling team. After practice one day, we were invited, separately, by some friends to a Tex-Mex restaurant. We bonded over being the only people who wanted to start the meal with tequila shots. A couple of shots and many drinks later, I had to drive him home (even though he claims that was his trick to spend more time with me). It was the start of a beautiful relationship.

Chapter 5: Trauma Healing

Love has a way of holding up a mirror, and when you're ready, it'll show you the pieces of yourself you've tucked away, avoided, or tried to outwork.

By the end of 2019, I was fed up with rising property taxes and started to reevaluate my housing situation. The house I was in (yes, the one I busted my budget to buy) wasn't going to work long term, not with two people working from home (we both worked from home *before* it was cool). Craig's lease was almost up, and I saw an opportunity: ditch the too-small, too-expensive house and buy something that would be big enough for both of us while lowering taxes. I was already in my thirties and I wanted to make sure he was "the one" ASAP. How do you confirm it? By moving in together, duh (this is a joke, it's definitely NOT the best way to do this!).

After the holidays, I quickly contacted my realtor and listed the house for sale. I probably drove my realtor crazy with all the questions and asking why we didn't have an offer yet after 24 hours. In my defense, this was my first time selling a house. I mean, I didn't know what I didn't know. And my personality is…if I wanted something done, I wanted it done right now. So the real estate selling process really tested my patience.

Everything worked out and we closed and moved out of my first house on March 10, 2020. The new house wasn't available for move in until March 16, 2020, so we were essentially "homeless" for a week. Remember what else happened in March 2020? Yep, the

COVID-19 shutdown. I had to stay in a hotel for a week while Craig took a business trip to fix equipment in a hospital in Austin. Not knowing too much about the pandemic at the time and whether it was safe to be out in public, I was super stressed for both of us. The fear of the unknown is so exhausting and all-consuming. I didn't realize it then, but our new house would become our bubble, our pressure cooker, and eventually, our healing space.

About a month after we moved in, one night, after dinner, I was bugging Craig about something (don't remember the topic) and I probably smacked him on the butt and Craig said something like, *"Stop it. It's like that's your personality."*

It sounds small, right? But that one comment spiraled me into a dark space I didn't know I was still carrying. I spent the rest of the night isolated, crying, convinced that I was broken and that my personality was flawed. All of my issues with self-worth and confidence came flooding back, and I genuinely thought, *I need to end this relationship before he realizes how broken I really am and ditches me.* I spiraled fast, and when Craig realized I was upset, he had no idea why but still tried to make it right. He started doing dishes (our agreement is the one who didn't cook does the dishes, and he is the chef of the house). It was supposed to be game night with his boys (every Saturday), and there he was, scrubbing away, trying to earn his way back into my good graces without knowing how he fell out of them.

Chapter 5: Trauma Healing

Then it hit me.

This wasn't about Craig or what he said. This was about my unhealed trauma. It was about my triggers, which were established long before I met Craig.

As a Military Intelligence Officer, I had been conditioned to believe that mental health care was a threat to my career. If you sought therapy, you could be deemed unstable, posing a risk to national security, and you would lose your security clearance and job. I remember at my last duty station, there was a Warrant Officer whose clearance had been put on hold (not for mental health reasons) and they put him in the company operations room to file paperwork. I was not going to let that be me. So I suppressed everything and pretended like nothing was wrong with me for my entire military career.

For the last three to six months of my time in the military, I was deeply depressed. I cried every day after work, sometimes for hours, and thought about ending everything. Not in a dramatic way, but in an "all the suffering would finally be over" kind of way (as you've already read, this carried over to my first years in the civilian world). It was the only way I could think of to get out of the current situation. I used to wonder, *how do people work up the courage to take their own lives? They must be so brave.*

And even though things got better after I met my tribe, trauma doesn't just go away on its own. It lies in wait to show up at the most inopportune times so it can continue to destroy our lives.

My trauma showed up mostly in nightmares. I had them about two to three times a week. Initially, I did not know they were caused by trauma; I thought they were just dreams because I had them so often. The nightmares would take place at different locations, but the theme is always the same. I would be in the nightmare by myself, looking for something—an exit, a building, etc. but unable to find it. Sometimes, it would be in a foggy forest where I couldn't find my way out. Other times, I would be in search of a building I could see, but I could not find the way to get there. I'm breathing hard, running, scared, thinking, "I'm never going to make it out and nobody is ever going to find me. This is how I die." I call these the "searching dreams."

When I was stressed at work, the searching dreams took place at my office, where I can hear other people talking but I'm unable to find anybody. I would open all the office and conference room doors to find emptiness. Then I would try to leave and would be unable to find the exit. I would think to myself, "If I can't find anyone that means they also cannot find me. This is how I die."

Remember the drunk driving? Yep, self-sabotage was my trauma response. Also, because I was so high functioning at work and social events, nobody would have suspected I had mental health issues

Chapter 5: Trauma Healing

including post-traumatic stress disorder (PTSD), depression, and anxiety (yep, I had the trifecta). It made it that much harder to seek help because it wasn't impacting my everyday life. Like a leaky pipe, it dripped slowly without anyone noticing and then one day, the entire roof comes collapsing down.

So why did I finally seek help? Because I owed it to myself to give happiness a chance. I refuse to let trauma control my life. And I owed it to Craig, who is literally the nicest Midwestern person I have ever met.

My tribe played an important role as well—those same powerhouse women first made me realize I had PTSD. I described what I was going through, and they told me it wasn't normal and that I should seek help. They showed me I am capable and worthy of healing. They also reminded me that healing was a part of freedom too. They made me realize that health is the #1 priority and without it, nothing else matters.

Because it was during the COVID shutdown, I had the mental health consult via a video call. This was the first time I'd spoken with a mental health professional, so I didn't really know what to expect other than what you see on television with one person lying on the couch and another person listening and taking notes. Well, this was not like that. It was a very matter-of-fact meeting where I got asked a myriad of questions about the trauma, when it happened, how it happened, what symptoms am I having, describe the nightmares, and a bunch of "on a scale of" questions. I had to relive my traumas all over again so the provider could report back to Veterans Affairs (VA) to let them know that it was service connected. At the end, the provider said I had post-traumatic stress disorder, depression, and anxiety. And then she asked how I felt.

There was a long silence while I fought back tears and tried to come up with an appropriate response to the provider's question. I didn't really know how to feel at that point. I just remember saying to myself, "Yep, it's confirmed. I'm officially broken." And then I started crying, badly. Like ugly cry, in front of the screen. Which is very rare for me. My tears usually only showed up for sad movies like the scene from *Tarzan* where he walks out of the treehouse in his father's suit and says to his ape mother, "You will always be my mother." Or in *I Am Sam* where Dakota Fanning testifies, "All you need is love." But when I heard the diagnosis, it was like every emotion that had been suppressed for the last ten years finally found their outlet.

After I gathered myself, the only words I could come up with were, "Okay, so what are the next steps?" The provider went through the process of getting me to see a therapist. She explained that it would also have to be virtual due to COVID. At first, I was skeptical. How could a therapist wipe away more than a decade of trauma, depression, and anxiety? But I tried it, mainly because I didn't know what else to do and I wanted to not be broken. The

Chapter 5: Trauma Healing

therapist recommended EMDR (Eye Movement Desensitization and Reprocessing) and I saw her via Zoom. She had me watch a light bar on screen and I was not able to focus or concentrate. Then we tried listening to beeps with my eyes closed and the therapist told me to imagine a light bar changing directions every time there was a beep. After the allowed sessions by the VA for community care, I wasn't seeing any progress. I still had the "searching dreams" about 2-3 times a week. Then Christmas and New Year's holidays came around and I took two weeks to go see my parents in Taiwan and never scheduled another appointment.

Then in the summer of 2021, my stepfather (who I will call my father from now on since that is how I see him), the man who raised me since I was about six years old, passed away unexpectedly. He had been in a multi-year battle with cancer, but just a few weeks earlier, the doctors had declared him cancer-free. And the day prior, I heard his voice for the first time after his tracheotomy. He called my Chinese nickname, Mei-mei, which means little sister. His health had been improving prior to his sudden death. His passing felt like a cruel twist of fate. On top of the grief, Taiwan was still under strict pandemic restrictions at that time and was not allowing any non-citizens entry without a business or humanitarian visa. That meant even getting to his funeral, to our mother, and to our family was going to be an uphill battle.

First, I had to prove that I was related to him to be able to apply for a humanitarian visa to attend his funeral. My mother had told us that he officially adopted us (my sister and me) when we changed our last name to match his, so I started digging through paperwork only to discover that the adoption never actually happened. All that had been done was a legal last name change. That revelation complicated everything. Our next strategy was still to apply for a humanitarian visa, making the case that we needed to be in Taiwan to support our mother through the death of her husband.

What followed was about two weeks of endless calls to the Taiwan Economic and Culture Office, trips to the post office for money orders, and expedited shipping of passports and stacks of paperwork. All with my fingers crossed that nothing would get lost in transit, specifically my passport. Finally, the visas came through and I had the passport in hand. But even then, we had to complete a mandatory seven-day quarantine in a designated hotel before we could see our family. I arranged for my father's secretary to drop off his filing folders and his iPad in my hotel room prior to my arrival so I could begin organizing his estate while I waited out quarantine.

My father had not left a will, but on his iPad we found a note in his "to-do" section to reach out to a lawyer to leave everything to my brother. His life insurance also listed my brother as the beneficiary. I honestly didn't think too much more about it, I mean in the Asian culture, the eldest son usually gets everything and takes

Chapter 5: Trauma Healing

care of aging parents, so it made sense that my father's life insurance would go to my brother so he could take care of my mother.

By the time we finished quarantine, it was too late to help plan the funeral. My mother had outsourced most of it to a third party. The timeline was tight: My brother's and my quarantine ended just two days before the funeral, and my sister was released on the very morning of it. We were literally writing our eulogies from inside our individual quarantine hotel rooms and Zooming each other for practice and translations. The emotional toll of being isolated while grieving your father is unspeakable.

On the morning of the funeral, several people arrived at our house giving us instructions about where to be and what to do. We were told that daughters could not participate in the procession that carried his urn and photo from the shrine to the funeral location across the street. It's customary in Asia to set up a shrine with the deceased's picture for people to pay their respects prior to the official funeral. The explanation was that since that would be outside, the girls should remain indoors to wait. I didn't push back at the time since we were rushing out the door, trying not to be late. But I remember the sting of being restricted by my gender.

During the ceremony, the children of the deceased will stand and return bows to those who came to pay their respects. They directed my brother to one side and said females go on the other side.

Another separation by gender. And guess what? The females got bowed to last, even though my sister and I were older than my brother.

After the funeral and cremation, it was time to move my father's ashes to the columbarium. The drive was about ninety minutes. My brother, as the eldest and only son, was given the honor of guarding the ashes in the lead car. I walked up, ready to join him from the other side of the car and provide support, when a family friend's son jumped in and stopped me. He said, "I will go with him, this is a male-only car." I said, "Excuse me?" He explained that only males could ride in the car transporting the ashes and that he was going to ride with my brother. And that's when I lost it.

I couldn't believe what I was hearing. They would rather place a completely unrelated man in that sacred car than allow his daughter to sit there, simply because I was female. I was furious. I told him flat out, "That's sexist." He quickly replied, "It's not sexist, it's tradition." And I shot back, "It's a sexist tradition. Those two things are not mutually exclusive."

This exchange wasn't happening quietly. It unfolded in front of 300 people who were waiting for the official procession to leave, not to mention the live stream on YouTube (because of COVID, the law only allowed 300 people to attend the ceremony in person so the third party who was managing the funeral opened a live stream for those who couldn't attend). But I dug in, ready to fight to the death

Chapter 5: Trauma Healing

for that seat, no matter the fallout. And honestly, if my mom and several of her friends hadn't stepped in and physically pulled me away, I would have won. I was 100% prepared to make a scene. Because at that moment, it wasn't just about tradition, it was about my father, my grief, and my right as his daughter to honor him.

When I returned home, the PTSD, depression, and anxiety came roaring back with a vengeance. I was back in that same dark hole as when I first got out of the military. The spiral started to happen again: Why didn't he adopt me? Why didn't he leave me anything? What's wrong with me that would warrant a parent of thirty-plus years not leaving me any of his estate? He must have never loved me. Am I always less than simply because I was born female? Will I ever be good enough? How can anyone truly love me?

I was having nightmares almost every night. The military trauma was now mixed with the trauma from my father's passing. The searching dreams featured me looking for my father, being able to hear him but unable to locate him. I would run throughout the house, opening every door, but nobody was there but me. I would be panting, sweating, exhausted. Then I would try to leave the house but I couldn't find the exit. Again, the thought would be, "Nobody's ever going to find me, this is how I die."

Come to find out, since my father did not leave a will, per Taiwanese law, his surviving spouse would receive 50% of the estate and his recognized children would receive the other 50%. Per

Taiwanese birth and family records, he had a daughter from a prior marriage who was eligible for 50% of his estate. Since my brother was born a U.S. citizen, he did not appear on the Taiwanese family registry. This new information provided some comfort. If my father didn't even want to leave anything for his daughter by blood, why would he leave anything for his daughters by marriage? There wasn't anything that I could have done to change this outcome. It wasn't me; it was how my father saw males versus females.

I decided to give therapy one more try. This time, I was assigned to a therapist certified in EMDR and was able to go in person. I didn't expect much given my first experience, but I needed to do something since my non-work life was pretty much falling apart again. I was blown away by the results.

This is what I remember from the sessions, though I will probably leave a lot of things out as this was several years ago. First, the therapist had me imagine a happy place. A stress-free place, real or imagined, that I felt safe in. She said that at any time, I could come back to this happy place. Then she handed me two paddles, one for each hand. The paddles alternated vibrating while the therapist gave me prompts to follow.

We worked on the trauma with my father first. She said, imagine you are on a moving train and your life is happening outside the train. So now think of your father and just let your brain continue to bring up images or life events. Every so often, she would say "If you

Chapter 5: Trauma Healing

want to share what you are seeing, you are welcome to" and at certain times, she would say "Notice that" after I told her what I was seeing in my mind. She continued to give me different prompts until time was up.

After a couple of sessions, I no longer had the "searching dreams" about my father. I would still dream about him every once in a while, but they were all normal, happy dreams.

Next, we worked on the military trauma. The setup was the same. We first reviewed my happy place. She reiterated that I could return to this happy place at any time. Then she said I should now imagine I was on a train and think about my military career. She asked me how I felt, what I saw, what I smelled, etc. A very specific image came to my mind of me standing in the forest at night, darkness all around me. All I felt was fear, and that I was going to die. Then she said to let the train start moving. Same as before, she would occasionally ask me if I wanted to share what I was seeing and then at times would say "notice that" after I shared. It took a few sessions but at the end, she asked me to pull up the original image and asked me the same questions: how I felt, what I saw, what I smelled, etc. It was amazing, I felt at peace. I could feel the wind on my skin, I could smell the trees, and I heard the movement of the leaves on the ground. She explained that our brains and our bodies remember everything, but we were so overcome with fear at the time the trauma happened that those memories were suppressed by fear. And once we reprocess the trauma, those memories are now available to us.

And just like that, no more nightmares. One week, two weeks, one month, two months. I was waiting for them to come back but they didn't. It was the first time I felt like I actually had a chance at a normal life. I am now a true believer in EMDR and that trauma can be healed. But it takes time, hard work, and vulnerability.

Healing shifted everything. I realized that to achieve financial freedom, I first had to achieve emotional freedom. What good was a dream life if I didn't love myself? If I didn't think I was worthy? No amount of money will ever be enough if you don't feel comfortable within your own skin.

Lessons from my journey to financial freedom:

Having trauma, depression, or any mental health diagnosis doesn't mean you're broken. It means you're human with significant life experiences that shape who you are. The CDC reports that almost 64% of adults have experienced at least one Adverse Childhood Experience (ACE). So you are not alone. The key is not to erase the past, because that's impossible. But we can learn how to heal and turn those experiences into memories that guide and strengthen you instead of triggering you. Healing doesn't erase scars; it teaches you how to live with them without letting them control your life.

Your triggers are your responsibility. The people who love you shouldn't have to walk on eggshells and in fear of setting you off. Healing means taking ownership of your reactions—not only so you can live the life you deserve, but also so those around you can live the life that they deserve too. When you start to heal, you'll realize that managing your triggers is not about blame, it's about freedom.

Trauma shows up differently for different people. No two stories are the same and no two healing journeys are identical. Just because your symptoms don't look like someone else's doesn't make them less real or less severe. It's important to talk to a professional, create a treatment plan, and stick with it even when it feels hard. Healing only happens when you allow yourself to lean into it. Healing is an active choice you have to keep making every day.

Create an estate plan. Whether it's a will, a trust, or both, this is something everyone should take care of as soon as possible, not just when you're old. If you own assets or have children, you need an estate plan. Otherwise, you're leaving it up to the government to decide who gets your assets and who gets to raise your children. Your estate plan will save your loved ones time, money, and potentially painful family conflict. It will allow them to focus on grieving and remembering you instead of fighting over paperwork and assets. Creating an estate plan isn't morbid, it's one of the greatest gifts you can leave behind.

Take time for yourself. Because I couldn't immediately leave for Taiwan after my father passed, I chose to continue working and planned to take bereavement leave later, once my visa was approved. But mentally, I wasn't in the right headspace. I found myself making uncharacteristic mistakes, like scheduling an interview but forgetting to include either the candidate or the interviewer on the invite. It was just too much, and my brain couldn't handle it. Even when you think you're fine, your body and actions will let you know otherwise. Listen to it. Don't ignore the signals. Rest is not weakness; it's a necessary part of healing.

The right people will stick with you through your healing process. Don't be upset if people leave when you aren't at your best. It means they aren't the right people for you in the first place. Those who stay and walk with you through the darkness are the ones who will support and be with you throughout your life. Treasure them!

Chapter 6
The Pivot: Untethering from Corporate America

"Money is just a tool that lets you do things. If you don't have a purpose for it, you'll start to wonder why you're accumulating it." – Michael Mogill

In the beginning of 2020, I hit a major milestone: a seven-figure net worth. I was officially a millionaire. I thought I was well on my way to achieving goal #2.

I celebrated. Briefly.

Then I went back to my inbox. Back to Teams meetings. Back to the relentless cycle of deadlines and deliverables. The "rat race" didn't disappear just because my bank account hit a certain number.

And that's when it really hit me: *Nothing actually changed.*

Sure, I had options. I kind of had security—at least I had an emergency fund that will prevent me from going into debt if something unexpected happens or I get laid off. But I still didn't have freedom, not the kind that matters.

How come, you ask?

Chapter 6: The Pivot

Because here was the makeup of my million dollars: Roth IRA, 401(k), an emergency fund, and two investment properties. The Roth IRA and 401(k) can't be touched until I'm 59.5 years old. The emergency fund is for emergencies. The two investment properties don't have enough cash flow to cover monthly expenses. Therefore, I was still tethered to a corporate job. If I truly wanted out of the 9-5 grind and to achieve goal #2, I needed monthly passive income to replace my corporate income.

So, I pivoted. First, I needed a better way to track finances. The Excel template was inefficient and took way too much time. It became a chore and was inaccurate because I would round and approximate. This led me to dislike tracking my finances. I knew I needed something that was simple, user-friendly, and that could automatically add up my income and expenses without me having to manually type in every line item. After some research, I found a free digital solution, one that would automatically pull balances from my bank accounts and group transactions by type. This software platform also gave me the ability to track my true net worth for the first time.

Now that I had an accurate picture of my finances, I started learning about investments that paid me *right now*, not just in retirement. I already had passive income from rental properties and the VA, but the cash flow was not enough due to having mortgages on the properties.

One way I thought of to increase passive income prior to retirement age was to grow my non-retirement brokerage account. This account not only focused on growth, but also on high dividends. The idea was that I would pull out the dividends and leave the principle so it can continue growing. I set up automatic contributions with every paycheck, starting with $250/paycheck. With every raise and promotion, I skipped the lifestyle creep and increased the amount contributed. Prior to my retirement in June of 2025, my monthly savings rate was consistently ~60%.

I also ventured out into riskier investments (after doing due diligence) and started investing in peer-to-peer lending. Private lending is not as complex as real estate. Essentially, you find a reputable company, give them your money, and in theory, get a return when the borrowers pay back their loan. But this was risky and there was no guarantee that I would get my money back. I'm not one to dive in headfirst—I want to dip my toe and test the waters first. So I started only investing $1000, which was the minimum investment amount. After a couple years, the overall returns were positive, and I loved that this was 100% passive income. After this positive experience, with more research and due diligence, I found a private lending capital fund to invest in. This fund is currently returning 8% passive income on a quarterly basis.

I shifted my mindset from building net worth to building freedom engines—income streams that kept flowing whether I was working

Chapter 6: The Pivot

or not. I made sure to create multiple streams of revenue that could pass *The Coma Test*: If you were in a coma, will the money continue to hit your bank account? If the answer is yes, then you're on your way to true freedom.

At this point in my life, I had six more years to achieve my goal of early retirement at or before I hit age forty. I had already set up the systems. Now all I needed was to invest as much money as possible as quickly as possible to take advantage of compounding growth. Where was I going to get this money? Through optimizing my corporate income.

Wait, you can impact your corporate salary? You don't just take what they give you?

Yes, you can absolutely impact your corporate salary and NEVER just take what they give you. Corporations are for-profit businesses. Every extra dollar they pay you is an extra dollar gone from the profit line. Corporations will always try to get away with paying you as little as possible. If you don't ask for a raise or a promotion, it's very rare that you will receive one. If there's one thing I learned in recruiting and HR, it is that the squeaky wheel gets the grease. It is up to you to find out your market value and fight to get paid your worth.

I'll share two powerful examples of how I learned to maximize my corporate salary, one tied to a promotion and the other to a raise.

Both experiences reinforced a crucial lesson: If you don't advocate for yourself, no one else will.

Example 1: The Promotion

In Q3 of 2015, I had been in my first civilian role for about fifteen months. We had been interviewing for a role on my team that would sit at another office. One afternoon, my manager called me into her office and explained that she was considering hiring one of the candidates at a level higher than mine. Her reasoning: "He needs the associate manager title since he'll be the only team member at that office."

That statement immediately raised a red flag for me. This individual had two fewer years of work experience than I did, and unlike me, he never managed people. By contrast, I had spent five and a half years as an Army Officer, leading soldiers in high-pressure and hostile environments. Leadership wasn't just on my resume; it was a core part of my professional identity.

I knew I needed to respond carefully. Instead of reacting emotionally, I calmly explained that it would not be equitable to bring him in at a higher level than mine. I reminded her that for the last fifteen months I had not only performed well, but I had consistently been operating at the next level. To make my case undeniable, I presented my receipts.

Chapter 6: The Pivot

- I had traveled to China five times in that period, stepping in as a translator for our R&D team and vendors because I speak Mandarin. Something that was neither a job requirement nor in my job description. And I did not get extra pay for this additional duty.
- One of our R&D project managers told me directly, "This project would not have launched on time if you hadn't joined the company because we couldn't communicate with the vendor."
- I earned the trust of our Chief Technology Officer (CTO) to the point where he allowed me to negotiate directly with our vendors. This was unprecedented; prior to my arrival, he always handled those negotiations personally and never let the sourcing team be involved.
- Through these negotiations, I saved the company over $1.5 million. Those savings were recognized with two formal letters of recognition from cross-functional company leaders.
- I received a quarterly financial impact award.
- And perhaps most telling of all, I was the only person on the new product development team who was invited to the national sales meeting, an invitation extended directly by the CTO himself.

In other words, I was already operating well above my title (remember when I said I was underemployed and underpaid...yep).

And I made sure my manager saw the full picture. Fifteen days before that other candidate was hired, I was promoted.

This was a turning point for me. It taught me the power of calm but confident advocacy, paired with undeniable evidence of performance. Promotions aren't just about time served; they're about impact to the organization. And if you don't articulate your impact, others will overlook it.

Example 2: The Raise

The second example comes from the annual performance review and merit increase process. For the second consecutive year, I received the highest performance rating. Along with it came a 6% merit increase, double the company's average of 3%. On the surface, this looked great. But when I ran the numbers, I realized I was still significantly underpaid. Even after the increase, my salary was still low in the pay band—about $17,000 below the midpoint.

I had anticipated this outcome, so I came prepared. After my manager walked me through the merit increase statements, I thanked him for the recognition and then shifted the conversation to share my concerns. I didn't beat around the bush. I told him that after two consecutive years of top ratings, my salary was still far below midpoint and it shouldn't have been. I'd been in this role for over two years and had four more years of experience than the role

Chapter 6: The Pivot

requires. At this point, I should have been positioned much closer to midpoint.

I was clear, respectful, and fact-based. Then I made my ask: "I'd like you to take my salary to corporate compensation and request an adjustment."

That conversation resulted in a $7,000 "mid-year adjustment" on top of my merit raise.

The fastest way to increase pay in a corporation is through changing roles (or changing companies) and receiving top performance marks on annual reviews. And don't forget about lateral promotions. Most people think moving laterally is bad or stalls your career, but it is quite the opposite. Lateral moves give you more experience within the company, open other potential future opportunities, and will net you more money. When it is time to move up to the next level, you will have a head start as far as salary is concerned.

Throughout my eleven-year career with my company, I had three vertical promotions (increase in level and pay), two lateral promotions (different roles at the same level but more pay) and at least two additional salary adjustments on top of the promotions and annual merit increases. My longest tenure was my last role at three years and four months (including a six-week leave of absence).

Don't stay in one role for too long, it's not advantageous for your wealth-building journey.

Bottom line though, is that you have to be a top performer. The promotion and salary increase conversations will go a lot more smoothly and most likely result in your favor. Because it would cost the corporation a lot more money to have to backfill you if you left. But always remember, if you don't ask, you won't get it. So speak up!

Lessons from my journey to financial freedom:

Net worth does not equal cash flow. If your goal is early retirement, you can't just focus on building net worth. You need cash flow outside of your retirement accounts. Your 401(k) and IRA are great tools for long-term planning, but the reality is they're locked up until age 59½ (with only a few rare exceptions, like certain 401(k) withdrawals at 55). That means if you want true freedom earlier in life, you need to create streams of income you can actually access and live on before then.

Optimize your corporate salary and benefits to fund your freedom. Every dollar matters when you're building your foundation. Fight for every penny of your worth. Corporations are focused on profitability. As much as they say they care about their people, they only care about their people because people drive profits. If you don't advocate for yourself and ask for that salary

Chapter 6: The Pivot

increase or promotion, nobody else will. Remember: The squeaky wheel gets the grease!

Benefits matter! Salary is only one piece of compensation. Benefits can hold enormous hidden value that adds up over time. Beyond equity and 401(k) matching (as discussed in Chapter 3), pay attention to the extras. For example, I never paid a phone bill for the first ten and a half years at my company. The only reason why I ported my phone to a personal account is because I knew I was leaving and wanted to keep the number. On top of that, I earned $685 annually, plus company swag, just for hitting milestones in the wellness app. That paid for groceries for two to three months for my household (both my partner and I worked for the same company so the cash from the wellness program pays for our groceries for almost half the year). Those "little things" may not look life-changing on paper, but over a decade, they stack up. Free money is everywhere, but you have to go and get it.

For veterans, make sure you research what benefits you are eligible for. The GI Bill and Yellow Ribbon Program paid for my doctorate. I only had to pay ~$600 in tuition, which was covered by BAH for that month. The rest of the BAH went directly into my brokerage account to continue to build wealth.

Retirement planning is more than having enough money to cover expenses. True retirement planning isn't just about making sure the bills get paid; it's about designing the life you want to live when you no longer need to work. Yes, you need enough income to cover housing, healthcare (including long-term care), and daily expenses, but that's only the baseline. Real retirement planning considers the lifestyle you want, the experiences you hope to have, and the legacy you want to leave behind (estate planning). Do you want to travel? Start a passion project? Spend more time with family? Give back to your community? All of that requires more than just "enough." It requires vision, intentional planning, and the right financial structure to live your ideal life.

Chapter 7
The End Game: Financial Freedom

"I can buy anything I want... but I can't buy time." – Warren Buffet

The day finally came. In December of 2022, my passive and almost-passive (rentals) income streams were enough to cover my annual expenses. The tipping point was when I received 100% disability rating from the Veterans Affairs which increased my disability compensation and exempted me from paying property taxes in Texas. The dream was being realized, but I wanted to make sure I didn't just have enough. I wanted to have more than enough in case something unexpected happens that would increase my monthly expenses permanently. I decided that I needed another investment property before I could officially retire. However, the interest rates were high, and the math just wasn't *mathing* to purchase another property with a loan—there would barely be any cash flow. Housing prices were also at an all-time high so buying with cash didn't seem like a good deal either. Deep down, I knew buying with cash was the only option for cash flow purposes. I was stuck between a rock and a hard place. Was the housing market

Chapter 7: The End Game

going to keep me from retiring early? I refused to let that happen. So, I put feelers out with my realtor partners to let them know that I'm in the market for a deal.

A couple of months later, a property came on the market that was being sold at a discount. It was an inherited property, and the heirs were looking for the fastest way to get it off their hands. It also needed a new roof that the heirs were not willing to pay for. The only way the numbers made sense was to purchase this property in cash since my goal was to increase monthly cash flow. With the interest rates being so high at the time, there would essentially be no cash left over if I purchased with a loan. But due to the increase in housing prices that happened during COVID, I didn't have the full cash amount on hand. My options were to not purchase or to liquidate a portion of my investment portfolio and reinvest it into this property.

Here's how I ran the analysis. I looked at my entire net worth and found that I was HEAVILY invested in the stock market (about 80%, not counting my primary property). And even though my stock portfolio was diversified, I knew there was an opportunity to rebalance and diversify into other asset classes. Now, it might have been confirmation bias at play because I wanted to buy this house but if I liquidated the amount needed to purchase this house, it would put my portfolio at approximately 60% stocks and 40% real estate. This was the portfolio breakdown that I was looking to build.

So I pulled the trigger and about 45 days later, I was the proud owner of a third investment property. It rented out soon after and boosted my monthly cash flow that made me feel more comfortable retiring early. The three rental properties provide about ~$45,000 of cash flow annually.

Now that the cash flow issue was taken care of, it was time to make sure my nest egg was going to grow enough in the next twenty-plus years so I won't run out of money in retirement. After all, I did just liquidate a large portion of my nonretirement brokerage that I had planned to use for retirement. I ran multiple models until age 99 and didn't get the number I wanted. The math said I needed at least another year of maxing out retirement contributions to ensure I never ran out of money. This was good news because I still had three more years before I turned forty. So I continued to max out my 401(k) and Roth IRA contributions.

But just when you think you're coasting, life throws a wrench. Craig and I were becoming increasingly displeased with the neighborhood. The neighbors did not respect privacy, and the HOA was getting more ridiculous each day. We wanted out. But financially, it was another tough decision. We had a 2.25% rate on the current house and the mortgage payment was under $2000. If we moved (this was in 2023), the interest rate was between 6-7%. Housing prices also had increased through the COVID years so our mortgage would drastically increase if we bought a similar house.

Chapter 7: The End Game

Craig and I had a serious conversation about the pros and cons of staying in this house versus buying new. And ultimately, we decided to bite the bullet and move because our mental health was worth more than any mortgage payment. After a weekend of searching, we decided on a new construction on an acre plot, no HOA. Our interest rate was 6.125% and even though we downsized the house, the acre plot added to the cost and almost doubled our monthly mortgage payment. We could easily afford this with our corporate incomes, but could I afford this in early retirement? Given that I only had three more years until my fortieth birthday, I made sure to quadruple check the numbers, estimating the ones that were unknown such as utilities. Everything looked good, so we gave it the green light.

We closed on the new house in January 2024 and sold the old house in March 2024. With the increase of housing prices since we purchased in 2020, we walked away with over $200,000 in equity after close that went directly into a brokerage account to continue the wealth-building journey.

Even though this move nearly doubled our mortgage, here's what it bought us: the ability to sit on my back patio without concern that neighbors were flying drones over my yard. The ability to play with my dog without having to take her to a dog park. The peace of mind of knowing that we're not going to get a letter in the mail because we went on vacation and were late mowing the grass by a few days.

After a couple months in the new house, I reran all the numbers to ensure I still had enough passive income to cover the increased expenses, now that I had the actual numbers from utility bills. Thankfully, the mortgage was the only expense that had increased. All bills either stayed the same or decreased because we downsized the house to get the land. The overall financial freedom strategy was still intact, and I did not need to increase my passive income.

So how do you know when you've made it? When you've crossed over into true financial freedom?

Here's how I knew. First, I had enough passive income to cover my entire lifestyle: all bills, vacations, spontaneous trips, and moments of indulgence, without needing to supplement with my corporate income and dip into my savings or liquidate investments. Second, my retirement accounts were in "coast FIRE," meaning I no longer needed to contribute to my retirement accounts. (FIRE is the acronym meaning "Financial Independence, Retire Early.") The money that I have in my 401(k) and Roth IRA will grow over the next twenty-plus years to last me until age 99. I can simply sit back and watch it multiply. And lastly, my entire corporate paycheck became discretionary income. I had it sent to a separate bank account to confirm I didn't *need* it anymore. I was consistently putting away ~$15,000 into investments each month. This is when I truly knew I had done it and that I can quit any time…or not. The choice is mine, and the world is my oyster.

Chapter 7: The End Game

Lessons from my journey to financial freedom:

Money is the tool, not the goal. Too often, people treat money as the finish line, as if hitting a certain number will magically solve every problem or bring lasting happiness. But money itself is meaningless. If you chase it without a plan, you'll end up with a lot of stuff (house, cars, bags) and a big bank account but you will be unfulfilled. Money is a tool to create the life you want. It's the means to your end game. The goal is never a dollar figure; the goal is living a life that aligns with who you are and what you value most. True wealth comes from living an intentional, purposeful life aligned to your values.

Chasing alignment. You can reach every financial milestone society says you "should," earn six or seven figures, buy the luxury car, own the million-dollar house, and still feel empty inside. True fulfillment comes from alignment with your core values, your long-term goals, and the life you've envisioned for yourself. Financial success without alignment can leave you exhausted, stressed, and disconnected from the very life you were trying to create. Alignment turns money from a measure of success into a tool for you to live intentionally and build your ideal life.

Financial freedom provides the foundation for the rest of your life. Financial freedom isn't the dream, it's the launchpad. It is more than a number in an account. It represents control, choice, and flexibility. It gives you the power to make decisions based on what you truly want, not what you have to do to pay bills and put food on the table. It allows you to leave a job or a relationship that doesn't serve you anymore, pursue a passion project, spend more time with loved ones, or invest in experiences that create lasting memories. Ultimately, it's about having free time to do what makes you happy and fulfilled. Financial freedom lays the foundation and is the beginning of your ability to live your ideal life. **The closer you get to financial freedom, the heavier the math.** When you're first starting out, the actual dollars and cents don't matter as much. Whether it's $100 or $500, the key is to get started and build good money mindsets and habits. But the calculations need to get more precise as you grow your wealth so you can actually arrive at your financial freedom number. Without the hard math, your dreams remain just that, a dream. With accurate calculations, they turn into reality.

Epilogue

July 1, 2025, was my first day of early retirement. Many people, including my mother, thought I was crazy to walk away from a $200K+ job at thirty-eight—the phase in life when most people have their maximum earning years. Also, the job market was terrible when I walked away. Economic uncertainty, tariffs, and AI were driving layoffs and causing people to be unemployed for three to six months or more. Most people did everything they could to hold on to their jobs and their incomes. I didn't need to.

The corporate job was always just a part of my financial freedom journey. A stepping stone, so to speak. It was never the end game. I did not have aspirations to climb the corporate ladder. When I first left the military, I told myself that I would work in corporate for ten years. Titles didn't matter to me; pay was what I focused on because that's how I achieved financial freedom.

Most people probably think I willingly retired. I did not. I *had* to retire because work was destroying my health. The burnout, stress, and mental strain which manifested itself through daily migraines. Yep, that's the truth—*Migraines forced me to retire.*

Although I was financially free, I was not seriously thinking about leaving the workforce until the year I turned forty (2026). In November 2024, I had daily migraines, and the searching dreams returned. Back in 2012, right before I transitioned out of the military, I also had really bad migraines. The Army prescribed me a narcotic and sent me on my way. After leaving the Army, I would occasionally get migraines here and there, but the prescription would usually take care of it. At the time, I didn't know what caused the migraines (I later learned it was triggered by stress and burnout) but since they went away after I took the medication, I didn't bother investigating it. I was also too busy trying not to be broke. But the migraines were different this time. The medication didn't work and I couldn't function during these daily episodes. I needed to root cause why they were happening.

About a year before the migraines got really bad, I got a new manager and about six months prior to that, I got a new VP. The team culture changed drastically. What once was a strong and close team simply fell apart. Our engagement scores plummeted over this two-year period. Personally, I felt shut out. I was always the last to know about leadership decisions and many times, I would actually learn about those decisions from my business partners instead of my manager, who sits on the leadership team. Many times, I would only get pulled in to fix mistakes or if a deadline was about to be missed.

Despite this, I did what I do best—*suck it up and drive on*. I worked harder, fixed others' mistakes, never missed a deadline, took on every project that came my way to prove my worth, driving myself to burnout. My confidence declined, and I started to doubt my own abilities even after I had gotten back-to-back top-tier performance ratings in role. I mean, why else would my manager not loop me in on important business discussions and decisions? It must be because I'm not good enough. I tried several different kinds of migraine medicine, did acupuncture, got a brain MRI, and bought new glasses.

I also went back to therapy since I had the "searching dreams" again. I saw a new therapist since I had moved about an hour away from my old house and we also did EMDR. It was similar to the last time with the vibrating paddles in each hand, the verbal prompts from the therapist, the "happy place" imagery. This time, after the sessions ended, I would still get the searching dreams but miraculously, I was able to find the exit or the place I was looking for. I was no longer scared, running, panting; it was like my mind knew where to go for the dreams to achieve a positive outcome. I'm not a therapist so I can't explain how it all works but to say I was blown away with the results would be an understatement. And the fact that each time I engaged in EMDR as a treatment, my healing elevated to the next level.

But unfortunately, nothing helped with the headaches.

Then, under the recommendation of my health providers, I decided to take a leave of absence to focus on my health. And magically, the migraines got less and less severe as leave went on. It became clear the cause of the daily migraines was work.

However, I still tried to go back to corporate. Why?

Epilogue

BECAUSE I WAS AFRAID.

Financially, I did not need the corporate paycheck. I had quadruple-checked my numbers and even ran it by a licensed retirement planner to ensure I would have enough money to last me until age 99 (the numbers actually showed that I would still have millions of dollars at 99). But *emotionally*, I was still tethered to corporate America. I've always had a full-time job. Who am I without the job, the title, and the multi-six-figure income?

But the migraines kept coming back, even when I was only working four hours a day. I literally had to lay down in a dark and quiet room for hours before the migraines would go away. It impacted my sleep and sometimes, I would wake up with a headache. I had several conversations with trusted confidants and they all said the same thing: your body is telling you what your mind won't—it's time to leave and take care of YOU. Your identity is not tied to corporate America. *Your worth is not defined by your title or salary.*

So I had a heart-to-heart with myself because for the first time in my life, *I had the option to choose not to work.* Which was also a new concept for me. If this had happened even one year ago, when Craig and I had just bought a new house at 6.125% interest rate and things had not stabilized, leaving corporate would not have been an option.

I also remembered what my acupuncturist, Dr. Kim, said when I told him about these migraines. "We work to live but the work is killing us."

As you already know, I chose my health and left corporate America in the rear-view mirror.

And that's the real power of financial freedom: *the ability to remove money from the equation and make decisions that are in my best interest.*

It's actually quite contradictory—we work hard to achieve financial freedom all so that we can stop thinking about money. But that is the goal. To not have to make money-based decisions. Because money-based decisions are rarely what's best for us mentally, physically, and emotionally.

With this newfound freedom, I am now focused on teaching financial literacy through JJ's Coaching Services—a space where I share the blueprint, demystify the process, and lead others to design their own exit strategy from the grind and create a life they love. Because financial freedom is not about money. It's about having choices. It's about regaining control of your future. It's about owning your time. And it's about becoming the author of your own life.

Acknowledgements

To My Parents:

Thank you for laying the foundation that made everything in this book possible.

To My Siblings:

Thank you for being my first teammates and walking beside me through life's ups and downs.

To Craig:

Thank you for loving the whole me when I didn't even love myself. Here's to forever.

To Mary and Paul:

Thank you for welcoming me into your home. You provided far more than just a roof over my head and food to nourish my body. Your kindness during my darkest hours provided an emotionally safe environment for what was a rather fragile mind, body, and soul.

To My Tribe:

You changed my life. I would not be where I am without you. There are no significant enough words to describe your impact on

Acknowledgements

my life. Just know that I will be forever grateful the universe allowed us to meet and become friends. Ride or Die!

About the Author

Coach JJ is a financial freedom coach, educator, and former military officer who helps high-earning professionals build wealth with confidence and intention. She holds a Doctorate of Education from Vanderbilt University, a Master's degree in Teaching from the University of Southern California, and a Bachelor of Science degree from the United States Military Academy at West Point. She is also a graduate of the Financial Coach Academy, the leading training program for professional financial coaches.

Born in Los Angeles and raised in Taiwan and the United States, Coach JJ is deeply rooted in both Eastern and Western cultures and is fluent in English and Mandarin Chinese. She began her professional career as an Intelligence Officer in the U.S. Army before transitioning to a Fortune 250 company, where she held leadership roles across supply chain, recruiting, program management, and human resources.

It was during her corporate career that Coach JJ realized financial success alone did not equal financial freedom. Determined to create a life of flexibility, comfort, and choice, she embarked on her own journey to financial freedom through finding her identity, trauma healing, and financial education. In less than seven years, she grew her net worth tenfold, becoming a self-made millionaire and retiring from corporate America at the age of 38.

About the Author

Today, Coach JJ combines lived experience, academic rigor, and practical strategy to help others build wealth without shame, fear, or burnout.

Contact the Author:
Dr. Jacqueline Jarl
jjscoachingservices@gmail.com
https://www.linkedin.com/in/dr-jacqueline-jarl-ed-d-35707b78/

Made in the USA
Coppell, TX
27 February 2026

72466410R00056